THE
ORIGIN AND SIGNIFICATION
OF
SCOTTISH SURNAMES

THE ORIGIN AND SIGNIFICATION OF

Scottish Surnames

WITH A

VOCABULARY OF CHRISTIAN NAMES

BY

CLIFFORD STANLEY SIMS

AVENEL BOOKS · NEW YORK

PUBLISHER'S FOREWORD

In order to add to the ever growing list of source books of genealogical material, we feel it is important to discover and publish volumes long out of print.

Such a book is *The Origin and Signification of Scottish Surnames*. First published in 1862, it lists several hundred Scottish surnames, with brief background information on their origins.

In reissuing this book we are pleased to make available additional research material for the genealogical scholar. This book was originally published in 1862 by J. Munsell, New York.

INTRODUCTION.

Scottish surnames divide themselves into two classes, Highland, and Lowland.

In very few instances were they assumed before the eleventh, and indeed by far the larger proportion, since the thirteenth century.

They have originated in various ways; are derived from localities, as Maxwell, Nisbet, Ralston; baptismal names, as Anderson, Bennett, Lawrence; trades, as Baxter, Fletcher, Nasmyth; offices, as Bannerman, Grieve, Walker; professions, as Clerk, Freer, Kemp; peculiarities of body and mind, as Fairfax, Laing, May; armorial bearings, as Cross, Heart, Horn; nativity, as Fleming, Inglis, Scott; and from many other sources.

Highland surnames are chiefly patronymics, with various prefixes and additions, as Farquhar, Mackenzie, Robertson; but there are some exceptions, a few being derived from localities, as Lennox, Murray, Ross; a good number from peculiarities, as Cameron, Campbell, Grant; and some from armorial bearings, and offices, as Frazer, Skene, Stewart.

Lowland surnames having been adopted mainly through Norman influence, are most frequently local, as Carmichael, Ridell, Rutherford; but many are derived from baptismal names, as Dickson, Henderson, Syme; from peculiarities, as Armstrong, Brown, Douglas; from armorial bearings, as Foulis, Heron, Lillie; from office, occupation, and trade, as Baillie, Hunter, Lorimer.

In the preparation of this work, the

author has been particularly indebted to the following authorities :

The Works of Sir George Mackenzie of Rosehaugh. Edinburgh, 1716.

British Family Antiquity, by William Playfair. London, 1811.

A General Armory of England, Scotland and Ireland, by J. and J. B. Burke. London, 1842.

A Dictionary of the Peerage and Baronetage of the British Empire, by John Burke. London, 1846.

A Genealogical and Heraldic Dictionary of the Extinct and Dormant Peerages of England, Scotland and Ireland, by J. and J. B. Burke. London, 1840.

A Genealogical and Heraldic Dictionary of the Extinct and Dormant Baronetcies of England, Scotland and Ireland, by J. and J. B. Burke. London, 1841.

A Genealogical and Heraldic Dictionary

of the Landed Gentry of the British Empire, by J. and J. B. Burke. London, 1858.

English Surnames, by Robert Ferguson. London, 1858.

A History of the Highlands, and of the Highland Clans, by James Browne, LL. D. London, Edinburgh, and Dublin, 1851.

English Surnames, by M. A. Lower, M. A. London, 1849.

Derivation of Family Names, by William Arthur, M. A. New York, 1857.

Surnames, by B. Homer Dixon, K. N. L. Boston, 1857.

Patronymica Britannica, by M. A. Lower, M. A. London, 1860.

In Scotland, whoever joined a particular clan, no matter what his position or descent, assumed the surname of his chief, and this was accepted as an act of loyalty; it does not follow, therefore, that all who bear the same surname are descended from a common ancestor.

Originally, all surnames had a meaning, but in very many cases this has been lost because of the corruptions in spelling, for their orthography has only been fixed in the last two centuries.

It is, therefore, probably impossible to render correctly the origin and signification of all Scottish surnames.

Philadelphia, September, 1862.

SCOTTISH SURNAMES.

ABERCORN.

Local: from the village of Abercorn in Lanarkshire.

ABERCROMBY.

Local: from the parish of Abercromby in Fifeshire. *Aber*, a place where two streams meet, and *crombie*, a bend. The family are descended from Humphredus de Abercrombie, temp. Robert I.

ABERDEEN.

Local: from the town of Aberdeen in Aberdeenshire. *Aber*, the mouth of a stream, and *Don*, the name of the river on which the town is situated.

ABERDOUR.

Local: from the village of Aberdour in Fifeshire.

ABERNETHY.

Local: from the town of Abernethy in Perthshire. *Aber*, the mouth of a stream, and *nithy*, dangerous. The family are descended from Alexander Abernethy, temp. Robert I.

ACHANY.

Vide, Hannay.

ACHMUTY.

Local: from the lands of Achmuty in Fifeshire.

ADAIR.

Thomas, the sixth Earl of Desmond, while on a hunting excursion lost his way, between Tralee and Newcastle, in the county of Limerick, where he was received and entertained by one William McCormick, whose daughter he subsequently married. At this alliance the family and clan took umbrage, and forced him to resign his title and estate to his youngest brother. He died in France in 1420, leaving issue, Maurice and John; Robert the son of Maurice returned to Ireland, where he killed Gerald the White Knight in single combat at Athdale, whence he received the name of Adaire. He afterwards settled in Scotland, where he married Arabella daughter of John Campbell, Lord of Argyle.

ADAM.

Man, earthly, red. The families of Adam and Adamson, are descended from Duncan son of Alexander Adam, temp. Robert Bruce.

AGNEW.

Local: from the town of Agneau in Normandy. Agneau in Norman-French signifies a lamb. A branch of the family came into England at an early day, and some of them accompanied Strongbow to Ireland; others of the family settled in Scotland, where Andrew Agnew was sheriff of Wigtonshire in 1430.

AIKENHEAD.

Head of the oaks.

AIKMAN.

From *ack*, an oak, and man.

AINSLIE.

From *ains*, a spring, and *ley*, a field.

AIRTH.

Local: from the village of Airth in Stirling-shire. The family are descended from Sir William de Airth, temp. Robert Bruce.

AITKINSON.

From *At*, an abbreviation of Arthur, and *kins*, a child.

AITON.

The town near the water — from *ea*, water, and *ton*, a town.

ALDJOY.

Originally from Italy. Peter Aldjoy obtained the lands of Easter Walkinshaw, by marrying, in 1547, the heiress Marion Morton.

ALEXANDER.

A benefactor. The family are descended from Alexander Macdonald, a great-grandson of Somerled, Thane of Argyle.

ALLAN.

From *aluinn*, fair, handsome.

ANDERSON.

The son of Andrew, which signifies a brave man.

ANGUS.

Local: from the county of Angus.

ANNAND.

Local: from the river Annan. *Aon, aon,* one and one, the river that divides the dale into two shares.

ANSTRUTHER.

Local: from the parish of Anstruther in Fifeshire. The word Anstruther signifies a marsh, or swamp. The family are descended from William de Candela, Lord of the lands of Anstruther, temp. David I.

ARBUTHNOT.

Local: from the barony of Arbuthnot in Kinkardineshire. *Aber,* the mouth of a stream, *both,* a dwelling, and *neth,* a stream that descends; *aberbothneth,* the house near the conflux of the stream. The family are descended from Hugh de Arbuthnot, 1160.

ARCHIBALD.

Powerful, bold.

ARCHIE.

The diminutive of Archibald.

ARESKINE.

Vide, Erskine.

ARMOUR.

Contracted from armorer, a maker of armor.

ARMSTRONG.

The Armstrongs derive their surname from the following circumstance : an ancient king of Scotland having his horse killed under him in battle, was immediately remounted by Fairbairn his armor-bearer. For this timely assistance the king amply rewarded him with lands on the borders, and to perpetuate the memory of so important a service, as well as the manner in which it was performed (for Fairbairn took the king by the thigh and set him on his saddle), his royal master gave him the appellation of Armstrang, and assigned him for a crest, an armed hand and arm, in the left hand a leg and foot in armor, couped at the thigh, all proper. The chief of the clan in the early part of the sixteenth century was John Armstrong of Gilnockie; he was hung as a freebooter by James V, in 1529. The family have always been noted for their courage and daring. In the *Lay of the Last Minstrel*, the chief when about to assemble his clans, says to the heralds,

" Ye need not go to Liddisdale,
For when they see the blazing bale
Elliots and Armstrongs never fail."

ARNUT.

The family descend from Michael Arnott, temp. Malcolm IV, and were seated in Fifeshire early in the twelfth century. The name has also been written Arnet and Arnett.

ATHOL.

Local: from a district of Perthshire. *Ath*, a ford, and *al*, a rock.

AUCHENLECK.

Local: from the parish of Auchenleck in Ayrshire. *Ach*, a mound, and *leac*, a flat stone. Auchenleck appears to have been a place where the Druids held their services. The family are descended from Sir John Auchenleck, 1450.

AUCHTERLONY.

The height of the meadow or marsh.

BAILLIE.

A bailiff.

BAIN.

White, fair, pale.

BAIRD.

An old tradition in this family records that William the Lion, while hunting in one of the southwest counties, happening to wander from his attendants, was alarmed by the approach of a wild boar, and calling out for assistance, a gentleman of the name of Baird, who had followed the king, came up and had the good fortune to slay the object of the monarch's alarm. For this signal service, William conferred upon his deliverer large grants of lands, and assigned him for his coat of arms, a boar passant, and for his motto: "Dominus fecit," which arms are to be seen upon an ancient monument of the Bairds of Auchmedden in the churchyard of Banff.

BALFOUR.

Local: from the castle and barony of Balfour near the junction of the rivers Or and Leven. The family are descended from Sir Michael de Balfour, temp. William the Lion.

BALLANTINE.

Local: from *Baalen*, and *teine*, fire, the fire of Baal. A place where Bal, or Belus, was worshiped by the Celts.

BANNATYNE.

A hill where fires were kindled.

BANNERMAN.

Assumed because of the family being hereditary standard bearers to the king; they bear in their arms a banner displayed argent, on a canton azure, St. Andrew's cross.

BARBER.

A dresser of the hair and beard.

BARCLAY.

Originally Berkely. The name signifies a birchfield, and was assumed from the town of Berkely in Gloucestershire. Roger de Berkely, a Saxon living at the time of the conquest was the grandfather of Theobald de Berkely, who settled in Scotland, and was the ancester of the Barclays.

BARON.

A valiant man.

BARR.

Local: from the parish of Barr in Ayrshire.

BAXTER.

A baker.

BELSCHES.

Local: From the barony of Belsches in Roxburghshire. The name has been written Belasis, Belases, Belshes, Belshaes, and Belsches. The family are descended from Ralph de Belasyse in Durham, who was settled there soon after the Conquest.

BENNETT.

A contraction of Benedict, from *Benedictus*, blessed.

BETHUNE.

Local: from the town of Bethune in France.

The Scottish branch of the family are descended from Robert de Bethune who came to Scotland in 1165.

BIGGAR.

Local: from the town of Biggar in Lanarkshire.

BINNEY.

The hill near the water — from *bin*, a hill, and *ea*, water.

BINNING.

The family bear a wagon in their arms because of one of them having, temp. David II, gone as leader of a party in a wagon, covered with hay, and surprised and taken from the English the Castle of Linlithgow.

BIRNEY.

Local: from the parish of Birney in Elginshire.

BLACKADER.

Local: from the lands of Blackader in Berwickshire — they bear an adder sable for their crest.

BLACKBURN.

The black stream.

BLACKWOOD.

Local: from the lands of Blackwood in Lanarkshire.

BLAIR.

A cleared plain, and as this was often the ground selected for combats and battles, Blair came to signify a battle. The family are descended from William de Blair, 1205.

BOGLE.

A goblin.

BONAR.

Local: from Bonare in Perthshire. The family are descended from Sir William de Bonare, Baron of Bonare, temp. William the Lion.

BORROWMEN.

A carrier of barrows.

BORTHWICK.

Local: from the lands of Borthwick on Borthwick Water in Selkirkshire. The family are descended from Thomas de Borthwick, temp. David II.

BOSWELL.

Local: from *bosch*, a wood, and *ville*, a village. The family was established in Scotland, temp. David I.

BOWMAN.

An archer. The family bear a bow in their arms, and also in their crest.

BOYD.

Fair complexioned. The family are descended from Robert, surnamed Boyt on account of his fair complexion, living in 1205; he was the son of Simon the third son of Allan, Lord Stewart of Scotland.

BOYES.

Originally Bois — a wood, a forest.

BRANDER.

A gridiron.

BRASH.

A rash or eruption.

BRIMMER.

A passionate man, from *brim*, to be violent.

BRISBANE.

A place where courts were held; *brys*, a trial at law, and *bann*, a mount; *breasban*, the royal mount. The family of Brisbane is of considerable antiquity; the present descendants are in possession of an elbow chair made of oak, having the family arms, with the date 1357 carved on the back.

BRODIE.

Local: from the lands of Brodie in Morayshire. The name signifies a precipice. The family are descended from Malcolm, Thane of Brodie, temp. Alexander III.

BROOKS.

A small river.

BROWN.

Originally Broun, and le Brun — dark complexioned. The family have been free Barons of Colstoun in Haddingtonshire, since 1116.

BRUCE.

Local: from Bruys in Normandy; Robert de Bruys was one of the followers of William the Conqueror, and received from that monarch grants of ninety-four lordships in Yorkshire; his son Robert de Brus obtained from David I the lands of Annandale, and was the ancestor of the Scottish family of Bruce.

BUCHAN.

Local: from the district of Buchan in Aberdeenshire.

BUCHANAN.

Local: from the parish of Buchanan in Stirlingshire. The family are descended from Macoum de Boquhanan, whose name is on the Ragman's Roll, 1296.

BURN.

A brook.

BURNSIDE.

The banks of a brook.

BURNETT.

A little brook. The family is of Saxon origin, but the Scottish branch have been seated for more than five centuries in the north of Scotland, and are descended from Robert Burnard, 1128. They bear a hunting horn in their arms, indicative of their office of king's foresters in the north.

CADDELL.

Warlike.

CADER.

A keep, a fortress, a stronghold.

CAIRNE.

A circular mound of stones.

CALDER.

Local : from the village of Calder in Nairn-shire. The family are descended from Hugh son of Alexander Calder, 1440.

CALDERWOOD.

Local: from the lands of Calderwood in the parish of Kilbride, Lanarkshire. The family were seated at Calderwood at a remote period. The last of the family were three brothers and a sister; and the former having quarreled with the priest of the parish fled to the Earl of Cassilis for protection, who gave them the farms of Peacockbank, and Moss-side, in the parish of Stewarton, and the Forty acre lands in Kyle. These three brothers were the ancestors of the present families of Calderwood. The sister remained in Kilbride, married a Maxwell, and became possessed of her father's estate.

CALDWELL.

From *colwold*, the hazel wood.

CALLENDER.

Local: from the village of Callender in Perthshire.

CAMERON.

Crooked nose — from *cam*, crooked, and *sron*, a nose. The clan have a tradition that their ancestor was a younger son of one of the Kings of Denmark, who assisted at the restoration of Fergus II, in 404, and was called Cameron from his crooked nose. Allan surnamed Mac Ochtry, or son of Uchtred, is mentioned by tradition as the chief of the Camerons in the time of Robert II. As far back as can be traced the clan had its seat in Lochabar, and appear to have been first connected with the house of Islay in the time of Robert Bruce, from whom Angus Og received a grant of Lochabar. The clan's more modern possessions of Lochiel and Locharkaig, on the west side of the Lochy, were granted by the Lord of the Isles to the founder of the clan Ranald, from whose descendants they passed to the Camerons. The clan appears to have been originally divided into three Septs: 1. The

Camerons or Mac Martins of Letterfinlay; 2. The Camerons or Macguillonies of Strone; and 3. The Camerons or Macsorlies of Glennevis. The Camerons of Strone were the ancestors of those of Lochiel — Donald Dhu, grandson of Allan Mac Ochtry, headed the clan at the battle of Harlaw in 1411. From this Donald Dhu the Camerons received their patronymic of Mac Dhonnill Duibh, or Mac Connel Duy, the son of Black Donald.

CAMPBELL.

Crooked mouth — from *cam*, crooked, and *beul*, the mouth. The family can be traced to the beginning of the fifth century, and are said to have been possessed of Lochore in Argyleshire in the time of Fergus II. Sir Colin Campbell of Lochore, temp. Robert Bruce, was called Sir Colin More, or great.

CARMICHAEL.

Local: from the barony of Carmichael in Lanarkshire. The family are descended from William de Carmichael, temp. David Bruce. Sir John Carmichael of Carmichael accompanied Archibald Earl of Douglas to the assistance of Charles VI of France; he distinguished himself in the battle of Beaugè by dismounting the Duke of Clarence, the English general, in doing which he broke his lance, and thus originated the crest of the family.

CARNEGIE.

Local: from the lands of Carnegie in Forfarshire. The family were originally proprietors of the lands of Balinaird in Forfarshire, but in the time of David II, John de Balinaird having obtained a grant of the lands of Carnegie, changed his surname.

CARR.

Vide, Kerr.

CARSON.

The son of Carr, or Kerr.

CARRUTHERS.

The family are descended from William Carruthers of Howmains in Annandale, temp. David II.

CASSE.

To oppose.

CATHCART.

Local: from the parish of Cathcart in Renfrewshire. The parish is situated where the river Cart runs through a narrow channel, and *caeth* signifies a strait; whence the name has originated. The family are descended from Sir Reynold de Kathcart, a Crusader, temp. Richard I.

CAY.

A place of security, a warden or keeper; they bear in their arms a griffin's head erased, in the beak a key azure.

CHALMERS.

One of the clan Cameron going to France, put his name into a Latin dress by calling himself Camerario, which in French is de la Chambre; upon his return home he was, according to Scottish dialect, called Chalmers. The arms of the family were cut on stone and wood in St. Nicholas' church at Aberdeen, with the dates 1313 and 1413.

CHAMBERS.

Vide Chalmers.

CHAPMAN.

A shopkeeper, a trader.

CHARTERIS.

The family are descended from Robert de Charteris, temp. Malcolm IV.

CHEYNE.

An oak tree — from *chene*.

CHRISTIE.

A diminutive of Christopher, which signifies Christ's carrier.

CLELAND.

Local : From the lands of Cleland in Lanarkshire. James Cleland of that ilk was the associate of Wallace, and received from Robert Bruce several lands in the barony of Calder. He was the ancestor of William Cleland of that ilk, who by Jean his wife, daughter of William Lord Somerville, was progenitor of the Clelands of Cleland, Faskine, Monkland, and Cartness. The family arms are derived from the office they held of hereditary foresters to the Earls of Douglass.

CLERK.

A clergyman. The family are descended from Alanus Clerk, living in 1349. The family estate of Pennycuick is held by a singular tenure, the proprietor being bound to sit upon a large rock called the Buckstane, and wind three blasts of a horn, when the king shllmoa ce to hunt upon the Borough Muir, near Edinburgh. Hence the crest, and the motto: "Free for a blast."

COCHRAN.

Local: From the barony of Cochran in Renfrewshire. The family are descended from Walden de Cochran, temp. Alexander III.

COCK.

The family bear a cock gules in their arms, whence probably the name.

COCKBURN.

The hill by the brook, from *cock*, a hill, and *burn*, a brook. The family are descended from Thomas de Cockburn, temp. Robert Bruce, their arms are argent, three cocks gules; crest, a cock crowing; motto, "Accendit cantu."

COLLISONE.

The son of Colin — *cuilein*, darling.

COLQUOHOUN.

Local: from the lands of Colquhoun, which were granted by Alexander II to Umphred de Kirkpatrick, whose son was styled Ingelram de Colquhoun, and was the ancestor of the family.

COLVILLE.

The town in the defile — from *col*, a defile, and *ville*, a town. Gilbert de Colavilla or Colvyle was a commander in the army of William the Conqueror; his descendant Philip de Colvill, temp. William the Lion, was the founder of the Scottish branch of the family.

COMBE.

The family bear three combs argent in their arms, whence probably the name.

CONGALTON.

The family are descended from William de Congalton of that ilk, temp. William the Lion.

COOPER.

Local : from the town of Coupar in Fifeshire. The family are descended from Simon Cooper, 1296.

COLLIER.

This name was assumed by an ancestor of the family, because when hotly pursued by his enemies he hid himself in a coal pit.

CORRIE.

Local: from the town of Corrie in the Isle of Arran.

COWAN.

A blacksmith.

CRAICK.

To storm — their arms are, per fesse argent and sable, a ship or, sails of the first; crest, an anchor proper; motto, " Providence."

CRAIG.

A rock, a crag.

CRANSTOUN.

Local: from the parish of Cranstoun in Edinburghshire. The family have been long seated on the Border, and their motto, " Ye shall want ere I want," was emblematical of their early calling of freebooters. They are descended from Elfric de Cranstoun, temp. William the Lion.

CRAW.

A crow. They bear three crows argent in their arms.

CRAWFORD.

Local: from the barony of Crawford in Lanarkshire — *cru*, bloody, and *ford*, a pass. The family are descended from Reginald de Crawford, living in the beginning of the twelfth century, who was the youngest son of Alan fourth Earl of Richmond.

CRICHTON.

The castle of plunder — *creachton*. The family are descended from William de Crichton, 1240.

CROCKETT.

Crooked, bent.

CROSS.

The family bear a cross crosslet in their arms, whence probably the name.

CRUIKSHANK.

Crooked legs.

CULLEN.

Local: from the town of Cullen in Banffshire — *cul*, a neck, *lin*, a lake; the place at the neck of the lake.

CUMMING.

A corruption of Comeyn, anciently de Com-minges, from Comminges in France. The badge of the family is the cumin-plant, and their arms are azure three garbs of cumin or. They are descended from John Cumyn, Lord of Badenoch, temp. Robert Bruce.

CUNNINGHAME.

Local: From the district of Cunninghame in Ayrshire. Malcolm Canmore being hotly pursued by Macbeth took refuge in a barn, where a countryman called Malcolm the son of Friskin, concealed him by forking hay or straw over him; on the accession of Malcolm Canmore to the throne he granted to his deliverer the Thanedom of Cunninghame, and for his arms, argent a shake fork sable, with the motto, " Over fork over."

CUTHBERT.

Famous, bright, of clear skill, or knowledge.

DAILE.

A bushy vale.

DALLAS.

Local: from Dallas in Elginshire. The name signifies a watered meadow; *dail*, a meadow, and *uis*, water. Sir William de Doleys was living in 1286; in 1367 John de Dolais was Thane of Cromdale.

DALMAHOY.

Local: from the lands of Dalmahoy in Mid-Lothian. The family was distinguished as far back as the time of Alexander III.

DALRYMPLE.

Local: from the barony of Dalrymple in Ayr-shire. The family are descended from Adam de Dalrymple, temp. Alexander III.

DALZIELL.

This family bear for their arms, sable, a naked man with the arms extended proper, and the motto, "I dare," to perpetuate a brave exploit performed by one of their ancestors. A near kinsman of Kenneth II was hung by the Picts, which so grieved the king that he offered a large reward to any one who would rescue the corpse; no one, however, would undertake the enterprise; at last one came to the king and said: "Dalziell," which signifies, I dare; and he rescued the body and brought it to the king, for which act his posterity took their name of Dalziell, and the arms and motto which they still use.

DANIELL.

The judgment of God.

DAVIDSON.

The son of David, which signifies beloved.

DEMPSTER.

An arbitrator.

DENNISTOUN.

Local: from the lands of Dennistoun in Renfrewshire. The family have been seated in the west of Scotland since the eleventh century — in the time of Malcolm IV, one Danziel, probably a Norman, received a grant of lands which he called Danzielstoun. The family are descended from Sir Hugh de Danzielstoun, 1296.

DICK.

An abbreviation of Richard. The family are supposed to be of Danish origin, and to be the same as Van Dyke. William de Dyck, Alderman of Edinburgh, 1296, was the ancestor of some of the Scottish families of Dick.

DICKISON.

The son of Dickie.

DICKSON.

The son of Dick or Richard. The family are descended from Richard Keith, a son of Hervey de Keith, Earl Marshal of Scotland, by his wife Margaret daughter of William third Lord Douglas. This Richard Keith bore for his arms azure, three mullets argent, being the arms of Douglas, a chief or, three pallets gules, being the arms of Keith — his son Thomas Dicson, born 1247, was the immediate ancestor of the family.

DINNES.

Probably originally d'Innes, from the lands of Innes in Elginshire.

DOBBIE.

A corruption of Robert, which signifies famous in council, from *rode*, council, and *beorht*, bright.

DON.

A down.

DONALD.

A great chief.

DONALDSON.

The son of Donald.

DOUGLAS.

There is the following tradition in regard to the origin of the name. In the year 770 Solvathius king of Scotland, obtained a victory over Donald Bain of the Western Isles, by the assistance of a man who was unknown to him. After the battle, being desirous to see one who had done him so signal a service, he was pointed out to him with these words: "Sholto Dhuglass," behold that swarthy man. One of this family, Sir William Douglas, entered into the service of Charlemagne and was the founder of the family of Douglassi in Tuscany. Sir James de Douglas took the heart of Robert Bruce to the Holy Land, to commemorate which his descendants have ever since born a crowned heart in their arms. Before the death of Bruce in 1329 the arms of the family were azure, three mullets argent.

DOW.

Black.

DREGHORN.

Local: from the village of Dreghorn in Ayrshire.

DRUMMOND.

The back of the mountain — from *druim*, back, and *monadh*, the mountain. The family are descended from Maurice, the son of George, a younger son of Andreas, king of Hungary, who came to Scotland in 1066.

DUDDINGSTON.

Local: from the village of Duddingston in Edinburghshire.

DUFF.

Black. The family are descended from the celebrated Macduff, Thane of Fife in the eleventh century.

DUN.

Local: from the parish of Dun in Forfarshire.

DUNBAR.

Local: from Dunbar in Haddingtonshire — *dunabar*, the castle on the hill. Crinan, Earl of Northumberland, before the Conquest, was father of Maldred, Earl of Northumberland, whose son, Gospatrick, Earl of Northumberland, having incurred the displeasure of William the Conqueror, went to Scotland in 1068, he was there created Thane of Dunbar and Lothian, and his descendants afterwards assumed the surname of Dunbar.

DUNCAN.

The chieftain's castle — from *dun*, a castle, and *creann*, a chieftain.

DUNCANSON.

The son of Duncan.

DUNDAS.

Local: from the lands of Dundas in Linlithgowshire. The family are descended from Uthred, son of Gospatrick, first Earl of March, who in the time of David I received a grant of the lands and assumed the surname of Dundas.

DUNLOP.

Local: from the lands of Dunlop in Ayrshire.

DUNMURE.

Local : from Dunmore in Perthshire. The name signifies a black moor — from *dun*, black, and *mure*, a moor.

DUNNET.

Local : from the bay of Dunnet in Caithness.

DUNNING.

Local : from the village of Dunning in Perthshire. The name signifies dark offspring, from *dun*, black, and *ing*, a termination denoting children.

DURHAM.

Local : from the town of Durham in England.

DURWARD.

A door keeper.

———

EDGAR.

Happy, blessed.

EDIE.

An instructor, from *eddee*.

EDWARD.

Good nature.

EGLINTOUN.

Local: from Eglintoun in Ayrshire.

ELLIOT.

The family are descended from Sir William de Aliot, who came to England with the Conqueror; his arms were, azure, a canton or; crest, an arm and sword; motto, "Par Saxa, per ignes, fortiter et recte." His descendants settled at the village of Elliot in Forfarshire, and some generations later, in the seventeenth century, were seated on the border, in Liddisdale.

ELPHINSTONE.

Local: from the barony of Elphinstone in Stirlingshire. The family are descended from a German named Peter d'Elvinton, who settled in Scotland in the reign of Robert I, where he married Margaret, daughter of Sir Christopher Seton by Christian his wife, who was the sister of Robert I.

ERSKINE.

In the reign of Malcolm II, a Scotchman killed with his own hand Enrique, one of the

Danish leaders at the battle of Murthill, cut off his head, and with the bloody dagger in his hand showed it to the king, and said "Eriskyne," which signifies upon the knife, and also said "I intend to perform greater actions than what I have already done." Whereupon the king imposed upon him the surname of Eriskyne, which has since been contracted to Erskine and Areskine, and for his arms a hand holding a dagger, with the motto, "Je pense plus."

ERWIN.

Beautiful, fair.

FAAL.

A rocky place.

FAIRBAIRN.

A handsome child.

FAIRFAX.

Fair hair — from *faex*, hair. The family were seated at Torcester in Northumberland, before the Conquest, but afterwards moved to Yorkshire; and from thence some branches settled in Scotland — Richard Fairfax was living at Askam in Yorkshire in 1205. Motto: "Fare Fac."

FAIRHOLM.

A beautiful island.

FALCONER.

The family are descended from Walter de Lenorp, whose son Ranulph was Falconer to William the Lion; they bear a falcon in their arms.

FARMER.

A cultivator of the ground.

FARQUHAR.

An honest man; from *fear*, a man, and *coir*, honest.

FARQUHARSON.

The family are descended from Donald Farquharson, the son of Farquhar, Chamberlain of Mar, temp. Robert II, who was a son of Shaw Macduff, a scion of the Thanes of Fife.

FELL.

Fierce, violent.

FERGUSON.

The son of Fergus, which signifies a brave chieftain—John Fergusson, "Dominus de Craigdarroch" early in the fourteenth century, is the first on record.

FERRIER.

Local: from Ferrieres, a town in Gastinois, France.

FINNIE.

Sincere.

FISHER.

A fisherman.

FLEMING.

A native of Flanders.

FLETCHER.

An arrow maker — they bear four arrow heads in their arms.

FORBES.

An old tradition records that in 870, Solvathius Forbes married Moravilla, daughter of King Gregory the Great. Another account states that, one Achonacher came from Ireland to Scotland about the end of the twelfth century, and having slain a monstrous wild boar, took the name of For-bear, afterwards turned to Forbeas, and used a boar's head in his arms to commemorate the deed.

In the southeast corner of the parish of Auchindon, is a spring, called the Nine Maidens

Well, near which nine virgins were slain by a wild boar. The boar was afterwards killed by a young chief of the name of Forbes, the lover of one of the maidens. From this circumstance, the boar's head is now borne by the Forbes in their arms. This chieftain, who was named John de Forbes, was owner of the lands of Forbes in 1214; his son, Fergus de Forbes, was father of Alexander Forbes, whose son, Alexander Forbes, was the father of Sir John Forbes, who had three sons, Sir Alexander, Sir William, and Sir John: and from these three brothers are descended the families of Forbes.

FORESTER.

A woodman. The family are descended from Sir Adam Forrester, temp. Robert II; they bear three bugle horns in their arms.

FOTHERINGHAM.

A house supplying food.

FOULIS.

The name is derived from an ancestor of the family, a Norman, bearing three leaves, called feuilles, in his arms.

FOUNTAIN.

Assumed on account of residence near a spring or well.

FRANCE.

A native of France.

FRAZER.

The family is of Norman origin, and assumed their name from the three fraises or strawberry leaves in their arms. About the year 794, Pierre Fraser, the Seigneur de Troile, was sent as an ambassador by Charlemagne to Achaius, king of Scotland. He married Euphemia, daughter of Rahan, a favorite of Achaius, and from this marriage sprang the Scottish Frazers. The fact of Simon being the most frequently used Christian name in the family, has caused the name in the Highlands to be corrupted to Mac Shimes and thence contracted to McImmey.

FREER.

A friar, a monk.

FULLARTON.

Local: from the lands of Fullarton in Ayrshire. The family are descended from Godfridus Fullarton of Fullarton, temp. Robert Bruce.

FYFE.

Local: from the district of Fife.

GAIR.

An outcry, an alarm.

GAIRDEN.

An alarm hill.

GALBREATH.

The strange Briton — from *gall*, strange, and *Bhreaton*, a Briton.

GALLAWAY.

Local: from Galloway in Kircudbrightshire.

GARDINER.

A gardener.

GARTH.

A hill.

GARVIE.

Local: from the Island of Garvie in the Frith of Forth. The family bear three garvin fishes in their arms.

GED.

A pike fish. The family bear three pike fishes in their arms.

GEDDES.

The plural of Ged. The family bear three pike fishes in their arms.

GEORGE.

A husbandman.

GIB.

A contraction of Gilbert.

GIBSON.

The son of Gib, or Gilbert, sometimes contracted from Gilbertson.

GILBERT.

Bright pledge.

GILCHRIST.

The servant of Christ; from *gille*, a servant, and *Chriosed*, Christ.

GILLESPIE.

A prompt servant; from *speach*, prompt.

GILMOUR.

A great servant; from *mohr*, great.

GILROY.

A king's servant; from *roy*, the king.

GLASFORD.

The green ford.

GLASGOW.

Local: from the city of Glasgow in Lanarkshire, or the town of Glasgow in Renfrewshire.

GLASS.

Green.

GLEN.

A valley.

GLENDONWYN.

The family are descended from Adam de Glendonwyn of that ilk, temp. Alexander III.

GOODALLE.

A corruption of good hall.

GORDON.

A round hill; from *gour*, round, and *dun*, a hill. The family are descended from Adam Gordon, Lord of Gordon in Berwickshire, and of Strathbogy, in Aberdeenshire, temp. Robert Bruce.

GOW.

A blacksmith.

GOWAN.

A daisy.

GRAHAM.

Originally Graeme — savage, gloomy. The family are descended, it is supposed, from Greme, a general in the army of Fergus II, 404.

GRANT.

Swarthy, grey headed. The family are descended from one of the Clan McGregor, named Gregory, dicti Grant, temp. Alexander III.

GRAY.

Local: from the castle of Croy in Picardy. The Scottish family are descended from Sir Andrew Gray, Lord of Longforgan in Perthshire, temp. Robert Bruce ; who was descended through Anchestil de Croy, who came into England with the Conqueror, from Fulbert Great Chamberlain to Robert of Normandy.

GREENLAW.

A green hill.

GREGORY.

Originally MacGregor. The name was assumed by some members of the clan on being outlawed.

GREIG.

Hoarse.

GREIR.

A corruption of Gregor. Gilbert McGregor, second son of Malcolm Laird of McGregor, settled in Dumfrieshire in 1374; his descendants assumed the names of Greer, or Greir, and Grierson.

GREIRSON.

Vide, Grier.

GRIEVE.

A superintendent of a coal pit.

GROSIERT.

A gooseberry.

GUN.

A plain.

GUTHRIE.

Local: from the lands of Guthrie in Forfar-shire.

HADDOW.

Local: from the town of Haddo in Aberdeen-shire.

HAIGE.

A hedge. The motto of the Haiges, "Tyde what may," is taken from an old prophecy of Sir Thomas Learmont, called Thomas the Rymer.

> "Tyde what may betide,
> Haig shall be Laird of Bemerside."

HALKETT.

The name in the charters of the family is written both de Hawkhead and de Halkett, and was assumed from the barony of Hawkhead in Renfrewshire. The family are descended from David de Halkett, temp. David Bruce.

HALLIDAY.

The name is derived from the slogan or war cry of the family "a holy day, a holy day."

HALYBURTON.

Local : from the lands of Halyburton in Berwickshire.

HAMILTON.

Local: from the manor of Hambleton in Buckinghamshire. The family are descended from Sir William de Hambleton, third son of Robert Earl of Leicester, descended from the Earls of Mellent in Normandy. This Sir William de Hambleton having slain John de Spencer in a rencontre, fled from the court of Edward II, to Scotland; being closely pursued, he and his attendant changed clothes with two woodcutters, and taking their saws, were in the act of cutting through an oak tree, when their pursuers passed by, perceiving his servant notice them, Sir William cried, "Through." He afterwards married the daughter of Gilbert, Earl of Strathern, and received from Robert Bruce the lands of Kedzow in Lanarkshire ; and assumed for his crest an oak tree with a saw through it, and for his motto, the word "Through."

HAMMIL.

A house, a home. The family are descended from Robert de Hommyl of Roughwood in Ayrshire, 1452.

HANNAY.

A leader, a chieftain; from the Saxon, *hana;* the name is also written Hanna, and Achany.

HARRIS.

The son of Henry, which signifies rich lord.

HAY.

In the reign of Kenneth III, about 980, the Danes having invaded Scotland, were encountered by that king near Loncarty in Perthshire; the Scots at first gave way and fled through a narrow pass where they were stopped by a countryman of great strength and courage, and his two sons, with no other weapons than the yokes of their ploughs, upbraiding the fugitives for their cowardice, he succeeded in rallying them, and the battle being renewed, the Danes were defeated. After the victory was obtained, the old man lying on the ground, wounded and fatigued, cried " Hay, hay," which word became the surname of his posterity, and the king, as a reward for his signal service, gave him as much land in the Carse of Gowrie, as a falcon should fly over before it settled, and a falcon being accordingly let off, flew over an extent of ground six miles in length, afterwards called Errol, and lighted on a stone, still called Falcon stone; the king also assigned three shields or escutcheons for the arms of the family, to intimate that the father and his two sons had been the three fortunate shields of Scotland.

HEART.

The family bear three hearts gules, in their arms, whence probably the name.

HENDERSON.

The son of Henry.

HEPBURN.

The sweet briar by the brook — *hiope*, a sweet briar, and *bourne*, a brook. Sir Patrick Hepburn of Hales, eldest son of Sir Adam Hepburn of Hales, was created Lord Hales in 1467; his grandson Patrick Lord Hales, was created Earl of Bothwell in 1488, the great grandson of the latter, James, fourth Earl of Bothwell, was created Marquis of Fife, and Duke of Orkney, and married Mary, Queen of Scots, in 1567, but was attainted and banished the same year, and died in the Castle of Malmoe in Norway, in 1577. The family bear a rose in their arms — motto: " Keep Tryst."

HERIOT.

One who provides furniture for an army.

HERON.

The family bear a heron argent, in their arms, whence probably the name.

HOGG.

The family bear three boar's heads erased azure, in their arms, whence probably the name.

HOLME.

An island meadow.

HOME.

Local: from the castle of Home in Berwickshire. The family are descended from William Home, temp. Alexander III, the grandson of Patrick Home, Earl of Dunbar; their war cry was " a Home, a Home."

HOPE.

The side of a hill.   The family are descended from John de Hope, temp. Alexander III.

HOPPER.

A dancer.

HORN.

The family bear a buglehorn in their arms; and for a crest, a buglehorn azure, whence probably the name.

HOUSTON.

Local : from the parish of Houston in Renfrewshire.   In the reign of Malcolm IV, 1153, Hugh Padvinan obtained the barony of Kilpeter from Baldwin of Biggar, Sheriff of Lanark, hence called Hughstoun, corrupted to Houstoun.

HOWISON.

The son of Hugh.   The family are descended from John Howison, burgess of Edinburgh, 1450.   The first ancestor of the family and his son, were farmers, and rescued James I from an attack made upon him when he had strayed from his attendants, while hunting near Cramond Bridge, and having saved the king's life by beating off his assailants with their flails, held a basin and a towel to wash his wounds. For these timely services they were rewarded with a grant of the lands of Braehead, the reddendo in the charter being "Servitium Lavacri," a service that was complied with to George IV, at the banquet of the magistrates of Edinburgh in 1822.

HUNTER.

The family have been seated at Hunterston in Aryshire since the time of Alexander II. They bear three hunting horns vert in their arms, whence probably the name.

INGLIS.

An Englishman. The family are descended from Sir William Inglis, temp. Robert III.

INNES.

Local: from the lands of Innes in Elginshire. The family are descended from Berowaldus Flandrensis who obtained a grant of the lands of Innes in 1153.

IRELAND.

A native of Ireland. The family are descendded from Sir John de Ireland of Lancashire, temp. William the Conqueror.

IRVINE.

Local: from the town of Irvine in Ayrshire, which is situate on the river Irvine, originally *Iar avon* or west river. The family are descended from William de Irwin, armour bearer to Robert Bruce, who received from that king a grant of the forest of Drum, and his own arms, when Earl of Carrick, viz: "three holly leaves."

JACK.

A corruption of John, which signifies God's grace.

JAFFRAY.

A corruption of Geoffry, which signifies In God secure.

JAMESON.

The son of James, which signifies He that supplants.

JARDINE.

The family are descended from Winfredus de Jardin, 1153.

JEWELL.

Joy, mirth.

JOHNSTON.

Local: from the village of Johnstoun in Renfrewshire. The family are descended from Hugo de Johnstone, temp. Alexander II.

JUSTICE.

The family bear in their arms a sword in pale supporting a balance.

—

KAY.

Vide, Cay.

KEEN.

Bold, eager, daring.

KEITH.

The family are descended from Robert, chieftain of the Catti, who having joined Malcolm

II, at the battle of Panbridge, in 1006, was instrumental in gaining a great victory over the Danes, and slew with his own hand Camus, the Danish leader, which King Malcolm perceiving he dipped his three fingers in Camus's blood and drew three strokes or pales on the top of Robert's shield, and these have ever since been the arms of his descendants. In the year 1010, he was advanced by King Malcolm to the hereditary dignity of Marshal of Scotland, and rewarded with a Barony in Lothian called Keith Marshal, and also with the island of Inskeith in gulf of Edinburgh.

KELLY.

Local: from the village of Kelly in Renfrewshire.

KELSO.

Local: from Kelsoland in Ayrshire. The family are descended from Hugo de Kelso of Kelsoland, 1296.

KEMP.

A soldier.

KENAN.

White headed.

KENNEDY.

The chief of the clan. Duncan de Carrick living in 1153, was father of Nichol de Carrick, whose son, Roland de Carrick, temp. Alexander III, took the name of Kennedy, and was the ancestor of the family.

KERR.

A marsh. The family are descended from Ralph and Robert Ker of Ker Hall in Lancashire, who were living in Roxburghshire in 1340, when Robert Ker obtained from David II, the lands of Oultoburn, and was ancestor of the Kerrs of Cesford. Ralph Ker was the founder of the family of Kerr of Ferniherst.

KILGOUR.

Local: from the parish of Kilgour in Fifeshire.

KINCADE.

The front of the battle, from *ceann*, a head, and *cad*, a battle.

KINLOCH.

Local: from the lands of Kinloch in Fifeshire.

KINNEAR.

A chieftain.

KINROSS.

Local: from the town of Kinross in Kinross-shire.

KIPPEN.

Local: from the village of Kippen in Stirlingshire.

KIRK.

A church.

KIRKALDY.

Local: from the town of Kirkaldy in Fifeshire.

KIRKPATRICK.

Local: from the parish of Kirkpatrick in Dumfriesshire. The family are descended from Ivone Kirkpatrick, temp. David I. On the 10th February, 1306, Robert Bruce, in company with Sir Roger de Kirkpatrick and other gentlemen, met Red John Cummin in the Grey Friars church at Dumfries. A dispute arising between them, Bruce stabbed Cummin twice before the high altar in the church, and rushing out pale and frightened, said, on being questioned as to the cause of his alarm, "I doubt that I have slain the Red Cummin." "Doubtest thou?" exclaimed Kirkpatrick, "I make sure," and hastening into the church he dispatched the wounded Regent with his dagger. In commemoration of this action, King Robert conferred on the family for a crest, a hand holding a dagger in pale, distilling drops of blood, and for a motto: "I make sure."

KIRKWOOD.

The wood near the church.

KNOX.

A little hill, from *cnoc*.

KYLE.

Local: from the district of Kyle in Ayrshire.

———

LAING.

Long, tall.

LAIRD.

The lord of the manor.

LAM.

Lame.

LAUDER.

Local: from the town of Lauder in Berwickshire. The family are descended from Robert Lauder, a follower of Sir William Wallace.

LAWRIE.

Crafty.

LAW.

A hill — also an abbreviation of Lawrence.

LAWRENCE.

Flourishing.

LAWSON.

The son of Law or Lawrence.

LEES.

Meadows, fields.

LEITH.

Local: from the town of Leith in Edinburghshire. The family are descended from William Leith, temp. David Bruce.

LENNOX.

Local: from the district or county of Lennox, now Dumbarton. Egrith, a Saxon noble, who died in 1064, was the ancestor of-Alwin Mac Arkyll, who was created Earl of Lennox, temp. Malcolm IV, and was the founder of the family of Lennox.

LESLIE.

Local: from the Castle of Leslyn in Hungary. The family are descended from Barthlomew Leslyn or Leslie, son of Walter de Leslyn, a Hungarian noble, who in the year 1068, came to Scotland in the company of Margaret, wife of Malcolm Canmore. In crossing a river swollen by floods, the queen was thrown from her horse, and in danger of being drowned, when Leslyn plunging into the stream seized hold of her girdle, and as he brought her with difficulty towards the bank, she frequently exclaimed "grip fast," and afterwards desired that he should retain the words as his motto. He married the sister of Malcolm Canmore, and was by that monarch made Governor of Edinburgh Castle, Lord Leslie and Earl of Ross.

LICKPRIVICK.

Local: from the Castle of Lickprivick

parish of Kilbride, Lanarkshire. The Castle was from time immemorial possessed by the family of Lickprivick of that ilk. The family made a considerable figure long before the time of Robert Bruce; one of the descendants was printer to James VI. To this ancient family was granted the heritable title of Sergeantry and Coronership in the Lordship of Kilbride; the charter is dated 1397, and was renewed by James I, James IV, and James VI.

LIDDEL.

Local: from the river Liddel.

LILLIE.

The arms of the family are azure, three lilies argent, whence probably the name.

LINDSAY.

Local: from the manor of Lindsay in Essex. The family settled in Scotland, temp. Malcolm Canmore.

LINTON.

Local: from the parish of Linton in Roxburghshire.

LIVINGSTONE.

Local: from the barony of Livingstone in West Lothian. The family are descended from Livingus, a Hungarian, who accompanied Margaret, wife of Malcolm Canmore, to Scotland.

LOCH.

A lake.

LOCKHART.

The name was originally Locard. The family are descended from Sir Simon Locard of Lee, in Lanarkshire, who, in 1329, accompanied Lord James Douglas with the heart of Robert Bruce to Palestine, from this circumstance he changed his name to Lockheart, as it was formerly spelled, and took for his arms a human heart proper, within a padlock sable, and for a motto, "Corda serata pando," which signifies "Lay open the locked hearts."

LOGAN.

An inclosed plain. The family are descended from Sir Robert Logan, who in 1329, accompanied Lord James Douglas with the heart of Robert Bruce to Palestine, and thus caused the addition of a human heart to the armorial bearings of his descendants.

LORIMER.

A bridle maker.

LOUDOUN.

Local: from the barony of Loudoun in Ayrshire. The family are descended from Lambrinus, who received a grant of the barony, temp. David I, and from which his son James took the name of Loudoun.

LUMSDEN.

Local: from the lands of Lumsden in Berwickshire. The family are supposed to descend from the Stewarts Earls of Angus.

LYLE.

An island. The family are descended from Radulphus de Insula, temp. William the Conqueror.

LYON.

Originally de Leonne. The family came into England with the Conqueror. Sir Roger de Lyon settled in Scotland in 1098, where he received a grant of lands in Perthshire, which he called Glen Lyon. Afterwards John de Lyon obtained from David II a grant of the

baronies of Forteviot and Fergundeny in Perthshire and Drumgawan in Aberdeenshire; his
son, Sir John Lyon, was Secretary to Robert
II, whose youngest daughter, Lady Jane
Stewart, he married, and was created Lord
Glamis, made Great Chamberlain, and Lord
Chancellor of Scotland, and received grants
of the Thanedom of Glamis in Forfarshire, and
of the Barony of Kinghorn in Fifeshire, and
was authorized to surround his arms with a
double tressure in honor of his alliance with
the royal family.

MACADAM.

The son of Adam. The family are descended from Adam Macgregor, grandson of Gregor
Macgregor, chief of the clan Gregor.

MACALISTER.

The son of Alister or Alexander. The family
are descended from Alexander Macdonald, son
of Donald, whose father Reginald, was the son
of Somerled Thane of Argyll.

MACALPIN.

The son of Alpin. The family are descended from Kenneth Macalpine, ancestor of the Scottish kings.

MACARTHUR.

The son of Arthur. The family branched off from the Campbells about the time of Alexander III.

MACAULAY.

The son of Aulay. The family claim to be descended from Aulay, grandson of Aulay, brother of Maldowan, Earl of Lennox.

MACBEAN.

The son of Bane.

MACLELLAN.

The son of Lellan. The family are descend-from David MacLellan, 1217.

MACCRAE.

The son of the king.

MACDONALD.

The son of Donald. The family are descended from Angus MacDonald, son of Donald, whose father, Reginald, was the son of Somerled, Thane of Argyll.

MACDOUGALL.

The son of Dougall. The family are descended from Dougall, grandson of Somerled Thane of Argyll.

MACDOWELL.

A corruption of MacDougall.

MACDUFF.

The son of the captain. The family are descended from Macduff, Earl of Fife, temp. Malcolm Canmore.

MACEWEN.

The son of Ewen. The family are descended from Anradan, son of Gillebride, King of the Isles in the twelfth century.

MACFARLANE.

The son of Pharlan. The family are descended from Gilchrist, brother of Maldowan, third Earl of Lennox.

MACFARQUHAR.

A corruption of Farquharson.

MACGAURIE.

The son of Gowrie. The family are descended from Donald MacGowrie, a descendant of Gorbredus, the grandson of Alphine Ruodh, King of Scotland in 830.

MACGREGOR.

The son of Gregor. The family are descended from Kenneth Macalpine, ancestor of the Scottish kings.

MACIVER.

The son of Iver, which signifies a chief or leader.

MACKAY.

The son of the champion. They claim to be descended from Ymore, son of Donald of Strathnavern, a descendant of Achonacher (claimed as an ancestor of the family of Forbes), who came from Ireland about the end of the twelfth century.

MACKENZIE.

The son of Kenneth, which signifies a chieftain. The family are descended from Colin Fitzgerald, a scion of the Kildare family in Ireland, who in 1263 came to Scotland to assist Alexander III against the Danes, and he behaved so well at the battle of Largis in Coningham, that he was in 1266 rewarded with the Barony of Kintail, in which he was succeeded by his son Kenneth, whose descendants were called Mackennie, afterwards varied into MacKenzie.

MACKINTOSH.

The son of the first. The family are descended from Shaw, living in 1163, second son of Duncan MacDuff, third Earl of Fife.

MACLACHLAN.

The son of Lachlan. The family are descended from Gilchrist, grandson of Anradan, the son of Gillebride, King of the Isles in the twelfth century.

MACLEAN.

The son of Gillean. The family are descended from Gillian-ni-Tuiodth, who fought in the battle of Largs.

MACLEOD.

The son of Leod. The family are descended from Malcolm, son of Termod Macleod, temp. David II.

MACMICHAEL.

The son of Michael, which signifies, Who is like God?

MACNAB.

The son of Nab, which signifies the top of the mountain.

MACNEIL.

The son of Neil. The family are descended from Anradan, son of Gillebride, King of the Isles in the twelfth century.

MACONOCHIE.

Sir Neil Campbell of Lochow married a daughter of Sir John Cameron of Lochiel, and was father of Duncan Campbell of Inverawe in Argyleshire, temp. David II, whose son Dougal Campbell, was father of Duncan Campbell, who was called in Celtic MacDowill Vic Conachie. The surname of MacConachie was thus adopted by the Inverawe family, although the cadets still used that of Campbell.

MACPHERSON.

The son of Pherson. The family are descended from Gille Chattan More, Chief of Clan Chattan, temp. Malcolm Canmore.

MACQUEEN.

The son of Owen. The family are descended from the Macdonalds, Lords of the Isles.

Early in the fifteenth century, Roderick Dhu Revan Macqueen settled in Invernesshire, where he had received from the Earls of Moray a grant of the lands of Corrybrough.

MACRORIE.

The son of Roderick. The family are descended from Roderick, grandson of Somerled, Thane of Argyll.

MAITLAND.

Meadow land. The family are descended from Thomas- de Matulant, temp. William the Lion.

MAJORIBANKS.

Margery's banks. The name was given to certain lands from their early owner, Margery, daughter of Robert Bruce. The family are descended from the Johnstons, whose arms they bear.

MAN.

A servant, a vassal. The family are descended from Sir Walter Maign, temp. David Bruce.

MARR.

Local: from the district of Mar in Aberdeenshire.

MATTHISON.

The son of Matthew. The family are descended from Matthew, son of Kenneth ancestor of the Mackenzies.

MAULE.

Local: from the town of Maule in France. Gaurin de Maule came into England with William the Conqueror; his descendant, William de Maule, settled in Scotland, temp. David I, where he received a grant of the lordship of Foulis, in which he was succeeded by his nephew, Sir Richard de Maule, who was the ancestor of the Scottish family of Maule.

MAXWELL.

Local: from the lands of Macchuswell, now Maxwell, in Dumfriesshire. The family are descended from Herbert de Macchuswell, temp. Malcolm IV.

MAY.

Good, pleasant.

MELLIS.

Sweet.

MELVILLE.

Local: from the lands of Melvil in Mid Lothian. The family are descended from Galfridus de Melville, 1165.

MENZIES.

Originally Meyners, and derived from the English family of Manners. The Scottish branch are descended from Robert de Meyners, temp. Alexander II.

MILNE.

A mill.

MITCHELL.

Great.

MOFFAT.

Local: from the town of Moffat in Dumfriesshire. The family dates back to the time of Sir William Wallace.

MONCRIEF.

Local: from the barony of Moncrief in Perthshire. The family are descended from Ramerus de Moncrief, 1107.

MONRO.

The family are descended from George Monro of Fowlis, temp. Alexander II.

MONTEITH.

Local: from the district of Monteith. Walter, son of Walter, Lord High Steward of Scotland, married the descendant of one of the old Earls of Monteith, and became Earl of Monteith in 1263; his sons Alexander, Earl of Monteith and Sir John Monteith, were the ancestors of the family.

MONTGOMERY.

The name is of Norman origin. Roger de Montgomerie came into England with William the Conqueror; his son Philip de Montgomerie, who settled in Scotland, where he received a grant of the lands of Eaglesham in Renfrewshire and died in 1140, was the ancestor of the Scottish family of Montgomery.

MOORE.

Great, tall.

MORAY.

Vide, Murray.

MORTIMER.

The name is of Norman origin. The Scottish branch of the family are descended from Alanus de Mortimer, who in 1126, acquired the barony of Aberdour by marriage with the daughter and heiress of John de Vipont.

MORTON.

Local: from the parish of Morton in Dumfriesshire.

MOWAT.

Originally De Monte Alto. The family are descended from Michael De Monto Alto, 1252.

MURE.

The family is of common origin with the Moors of Kent, and also with the great Irish house of Moor. The name has been written Moore, Moor, More, Muir, and Mure. The Scottish branch of the family are descended from Sir Reginald Mure, Chamberlain of Scotland in 1329.

MURRAY.

A warlike tribe called the Moravii came at an early day from Germany to Scotland, and gave their name to the district now called Moray or Murray. The family name was originally de Moravia, and they are descended from Friskinus de Moravia, temp. David II.

MUTERER.

A collector of mill toll.

NAIRNE.

Local: from the borough of Nairne in Nairnshire. The family are descended from Michael de Nairn, 1400.

NAPIER.

King David II, in his wars with the English, about the year 1344, convocating his subjects to battle, the Earl of Lennox sent his second son, Donald, with such forces as his duty obliged him; and coming to an engagement where the Scots gave way, this Donald taking his father's standard from the bearer, and valiantly charging the enemy with the Lennox men, the fortune of the battle changed, and the Scots obtained the victory. After the battle, the king declared that they had all done valiantly, but that there was one among them who had *na pier*, no equal; he then granted to Donald the lands of Gosfield in Fifeshire, and bade him assume the name of Napier.

NASMYTH.

A nail maker — they bear two broken hammers in their arms.

NEIL.

Dark complexion.

NEILSON.

The son of Neil.

NESS.

A promontory.

NEWTON.

Local: From Newton in Haddingtonshire. The family were seated there in 1377; Sir Isaac Newton derived his descent from them.

NISBET.

Local: from the lands of Nisbet in Berwickshire. The family are descended from Philip de Nesbyth, temp. David I.

———

OGILVY.

Local: from the Barony of Ogilvy in Forfarshire. The family are descended from Gilbert, brother of Gilchrist, Earl of Angus, who obtained from William the Lion a grant of the Barony of Ogilvy.

OGLE.

Local: from the Ogle Castle in Northumberland. The family are descended from Robert Ogle of Ogle, temp. Edward III.

OLIPHANT.

An elephant — they bear two elephants rampant for supporters, whence probably the name. The family are descended from Sir Walter Oliphant, who married Elizabeth, daughter of Robert Bruce.

OLIVER.

Peace.

ORCHARD.

A collection of fruit trees.

ORD.

Point, edge.

ORME.

An elm tree.

ORR.

Local : from the village of Orr in Kircudbrightshire.

OSWALD.

A steward.

——

PATERSON.

The son of Patrick.

PATRICK.

A senator. The family are descended from John Patrick, 1459.

PATTISON.

A corruption of Paterson.

PAUL.

Little, small.

PEACOCK.

A name given from fondness for display — they bear three peacocks in their pride, in their arms.

PEARSON.

The son of Pierre.

PEEBLES.

Local: from Peebles in Peebleshire.

PETER.

A rock.

PETERSON.

The son of Peter.

PITCAIRN.

Local: from the lands of Pitcairn in Perthshire. The family are descended from Johannes de Pitcairn, 1250.

POLLOCK.

Local: from the parish of Pollock in Renfrewshire. The family are descended from Petrus Pollok, temp. Malcolm IV.

PORTERFIELD.

Local: from the village of Porterfield in Renfrewshire. The family are descended from John de Porter, 1262.

PRESTON.

Local: from the town of Preston in Haddingtonshire. The family are descended from Leolphus de Preston, 1165.

PRIMROSE.

Local: from the lands of Primrose in Fifeshire.

PRINGLE.

A pilgrim. The family are descended from William Pringle of Whitton, 1492 — they bear in their arms the escallop shells or badges of pilgrims to the Holy Land.

QUIN.

White.

———

RALSTON.

Local: from the lands of Ralston in Renfrewshire. The family are descended from Ralph, son of Macduff, Thane of Fife, who obtained a grant of lands in Renfrewshire, which he called Ralphstoun, corrupted to Ralston. The Ralstons of that ilk are mentioned in charters as far back as 1272 and 1346; and early in the fifteenth century John de Ralstoune or Ralphstoun was Lord High Treasurer and Bishop of Dunkeld.

RAMSAY.

Local: from the village of Ramsay in Huntingdonshire. The Scottish branch of the family are descended from Simon de Ramsay of Dalhousie in Edinburghshire, temp. David I. The Abbot of Ramsay bore on his seal a ram in the sea, with this verse: " *Cujus signa quo dux gregis ut ego;*" He whose signs I bear is leader of the flock, as I am.

RANDOLPH.

Fair help, from *ran*, fair, and *ulph*, help.   Sir Thomas Randolph was created Earl of Murray in 1313.

RATTRAY.

Local: from the barony of Rattray in Perthshire.   The family are descended from Alanus de Rateriff, temp. William the Lion.

REID.

Red.

RIDELL.

Local: from the lands of Ridell in Roxburghshire.   The family are descended from Oscitel de Ridel, 1090.

RIG.

Rich, wealthy.

RITCHIE.

A contraction of Richard, which signifies of a generous disposition.

ROBERTSON.

The son of Robert.   The family are descended from the ancient Earls of Athol, who were derived from Duncan, king of Scotland, son of

Malcolm Canmore. The name was assumed by Alexander, son of that Robert who arrested the murderers of James I, and for which act James II granted him for a crest a hand supporting a regal crown.

ROGER.

Peace.

ROLLO.

The family are descended Richard de Rollo, son of Richard, Duke of Normandy, and brother of William the Conqueror, who settled in Perthshire, temp. David I.

ROSS.

Local: from the district of Ross. Robert de Ross married Isabel, daughter of William the Lion. Sir John Ross was created Lord Ross in 1489.

ROY.

Red haired.

RUTHERFORD.

Local: from the lands of Rutherford in Roxburghshire. The family are descended from Sir Richard de Ruthirfurde, 1390.

RUTHVEN.

Local : from the Barony of Ruthven, in Perthshire.   The family are descended from Swanus
de Ruthven, temp. William the Lion

SANDERS.

A contraction of Alexander.

SANDILANDS.

Local: from the barony of Sandilands in
Lanarkshire.   The family are descended from
Sir James Sandilands, temp. David Bruce.

SCOTT.

A native of Scotland.   *Skot*, signifies a dart.
The family are descended from Uchtredus Scot,
1128.

SCRYMGEOUR.

A skirmisher.   The family are descended
from Sir Alexander Carron, temp. Alexander I,
who received the name of Scrymgeour, on account of his activity.

SEMPLE.

A contraction of St. Paul.   The family are
descended from Robert Semple of Ellerston in
Renfrewshire, 1250.

SETON.

Local : from the lands of Seton in Hadding-tonshire. The family are descended from Dow-gal Seaton, temp. Malcolm Canmore — their ancient war cry and motto was "Set on."

SHAW.

A thicket, a grove. The Highland family of Shaw is a branch of the clan Mackintosh.

SIBBALD.

The family are descended from "Dominus Sybaldus, Miles de Mearnis," temp. William the Lion ; his posterity, "Walterus filius Sybaldi," Mathæus Sybald, and others are frequently mentioned as witnesses to the Royal Charters. The motto of the family is "Sae bauld."

SIM.

Vide, Syme.

SIMSON.

The son of Sim, or Simon. Some of the families of Simson are descended from the Frazers.

SINCLAIR.

A corruption of St. Clare. The family are

descended from Walderness Compte de Saint
Clare, who came into England with William
the Conqueror; his son, William de Sancto
Claro, settled in Scotland, where he obtained
from Alexander I, a grant of the Barony of
Roslyn.

SKENE.

Some derive their names as well as their
arms from some considerable action, and thus a
son of Struan Robertson, for killing a wolf in
Stocket forest in Athole, in the king's presence,
with a dirk, received the name of Skene, which
signifies a dirk, and three dirks points in pale,
for his arms.

SMITH.

A worker in metals. The name is written
Smyth, and Smythe. Some of the families of
Smith are descended from Neil Cromb, third
son of Murdoch, Chief of Clan Chattan, temp.
William the Lion.

SNODGRASS.

Trimmed or smooth grass.

SOMERVILLE.

The family are descended from Sir Walter de
Somerville, who came into England with Wil-

liam the Conqueror; his son, William de Somerville, settled in Scotland.

SPENS.

The family are descended from William de
Spens of Lathallan in Fifeshire, 1392, who
married Isabel, daughter and heiress of Duncan
Campbell of Glen Douglas, in commemoration
of which the family quarter the Campbell arms
of gyronny of eight or and sable.

SPITTAL.

An hospital.

SPOTTISWOODE.

Local: from the Barony of Spottiswoode in
Berwickshire. The family are descended from
Robert de Spottiswoode, temp. Alexander III.

STEIN.

Local: from the town of Stein in the Isle of
Skye.

STEPHEN.

Honor.

STEWART.

Banquo, Thane of Lochabyr, was Steward
to Duncan I; the descendants of his grandson,

Walter, who was created by Malcolm Canmore, Lord High Steward of Scotland, assumed the surname of Stewart or Stuart.

STIRLING.

Local : from the town of Stirling in Stirlingshire. Sir John Stirling of Glorat, was armor bearer to James I.

STOTT.

A young ox.

STRACHAN.

Local: from the parish of Strachan in Kincardineshire. The family are descended from Walderus de Strathecan, 1165.

STUART.

Vide, Stewart.

SUTHERLAND.

Local: from the county of Sutherland. The family are descended from Allan, Thane of Sutherland, temp. Malcolm Canmore.

SWINTON.

Local: from the Barony of Swinton in Berwickshire. The family are descended from Edulph de Swinton, 1060.

SYME.

The son of Symon, or Simon. The Gaelic words *sema* and *syma*, signify a peacemaker. The word *syme* or *sime*, in old Norman French, signifies sixth. The first of the name found on record is Syme of Spalding, also called Peter Spalding, who married a cousin of the Earl of Dunbar, and was a Burgess and also Governor of Berwick, which town he delivered by stratagem from the English to the Scotch in 1318.

SYMINGTON.

Local: from the parish of Symington in Ayrshire. Originally called Symonstoun, from Simon Lockhart, who held the lands under Walter the first Steward.

TAIT.

Pleasure, delight.

TAWSE.

Straps for whipping.

THOMSON.

The son of Thomas, which signifies a twin.

TRAIL.

To drag.

TROTTER.

A rambler. John Trotter was outlawed, temp. Robert II.

TURNBULL.

The first of this family is said to have been a strong man named Ruel, who turned a wild bull by the head, which had violently ran against Robert Bruce in Stirling Park; for which act he received from that king the lands of Bedrule, and the name of Turnbull. He is called in the charter " Willielmo dicto Turn-bull." At the battle of Halidonhill, this Ruel advanced before the Scotch army with a great dog, and challenged any of the English to fight with him a combat. Sir Robert Venal, a Nor-folk man, fought and killed him and his dog too. The descendants of Ruel bore a bull's head in their arms (modernly three bull's heads), in allusion to the feat from which their name originated.

TYTLER.

In the year 1515, Lord Seton, having slain a gentleman named Gray in a duel, changed his name to Tytler and fled to France. His two sons returned with Queen Mary to Scotland in 1561, and settled in Aberdeenshire.

URQUHART.

Local: from the castle of Urquhart, in the parish of Urquhart, Elginshire. The family are descended from Gallerouch Urchard, temp. Alexander II. William Urchard of Cromarty was heritable Sheriff of that shire, temp. Robert Bruce.

VACH.

A cow — they bear three cow's heads sable, in their arms.

VERE.

Originally Weir or Were — a fish dam. The family are descended from Rotaldus Were of Blackwood in Lanarkshire, 1404.

VIPONT.

The family are of Norman origin, the Scottish branch being descended from William de Veteri Ponte, 1165. The name has been corrupted to Wepont.

WALKER.

An inspector of a forest.

WALLACE.

The family are descended from Eimurus Galleius, whose son Richard Walense was living in the time of Walter the first Steward, and was father of Henry Waleys, whose son was Adam Wallace of Riccarton, 1158.

WARRENDER.

Originally de Warren. The family are descended from Robert de Warren, who settled in East Lothian from Yorkshire.

WATSON.

The son of Walter, which signifies the lord of the wood — from *wald*, a wood, and *heer*, a master.

WEDDERBURN.

Local: from the lands of Wedderburn in Berwickshire.

WELLWOOD.

Founded by Velvud, a Danish courtier, who escorted Anne, Queen to James VI, to Scotland,

and received from her a grant of the lands of Touch, and the following armorial bearings, argent, out of a well gules, an oak tree growing, vert.

WEMYSS.

Local: from the town of Wemyss in Fifeshire. The family are descended from John, son of Macduff, Thane of Fife, who assumed the name from his lands.

WHITEHEAD.

Gray haired.

WILSON.

The son of William. The family are said to be descended from a Prince of Denmark, and were established at a very remote period in the Orkney islands, intermarrying with the clans of Monro, and others. After a long continuance in the north, alliances taking place with some of the principal Lowland families, the Wilsons moved southward. Motto: " Wil sone will."

WINTON.

Local: from Winton in Haddingtonshire.

WISHART.

The family are of ancient date in Forfarshire,

and are descended from Robert, a natural son of David, Earl of Huntingdon, who having gone on a crusade to the Holy Land, was called Guishart, on account of the slaughter he made of the Saracens.   Adam Wishart of Logie, was living in 1272.

WOOD.

Originally de Bosco — they bear an oak tree in their arms.

YETTS.

A gate, a way, a passage — they bear three portcullises gules, in their arms.

YOUNG.

A name given on account of age.

YULE.

Christmas.   The name was probably first given to one born at that time.

ADDITIONS AND CORRECTIONS.

ALLARDICE.

Local: from Allardice, originally Alrethes, in Kincardineshire. The family were seated there, temp. William the Lion.

AYTOUN.

Local: from the parish of Aytoun in Berwickshire.

BAIRD.

See p. 16. An old prophecy of Sir Thomas Learmont, called Thomas the Rymer, says: "there shall be an eagle in the craig while there is a Baird in Auchmedden."

BALDERSTON.

Local: from Balderston in Linlithgowshire.

BARCLAY.

See p. 18, line 3, for *ancester* read *ancestor*.

BERTRAM.

Fair and pure.

BOYLE.

Probably originally Boyville, from Bouville, a parish near Rouen, France. The Scottish family are descended from Richard Boyle of Kelburn in Ayrshire, temp. Alexander III.

BRECHIN.

Local: from the town of Brechin in Forfarshire. Henry Brechin was created Lord Brechin by David I.

BRICE.

Descended from Rev. Edward Bruce, a younger son of the Laird of Airth, who settling in Ireland early in the seventeenth century, changed his name to Bryce, since altered to Brice.

BRISBANE.

See p. 22. William Brisbane was Chancellor of Scotland in 1332.

BROWN.

See p. 22. The family claim descent from the Royal family of France, and bear for their arms, gu., three fleur de lis or.

——

CARLYLE.

Local: from the city of Carlisle in Cumberland. Hildred de Karleolo, temp. William I, was owner of lands in Cumberland, on which the city of Carlisle now stands. His descendant, Adam de Karleolo, accompanied William de Bruce, Lord of Annandale, to Scotland, in 1170, and received from him a grant of the lands of Kynemound in Dumfriesshire; and was the ancestor of the Scottish branch of the family.

CHISHOLM.

Descended from Harald Chisholm, Thane of Orkney, Caithness and Shetland, temp. William the Lion. He was a scion of the Royal stock of Norway, and married the daughter of

Mached, Earl of Athol, the last male descendant of Donald Ban, King of Scotland. The clan are called in the North, An Siosalach.

CLEGHORN.

Local: from Cleghorn in Lanarkshire.

CRAMOND.

Local: from the village of Cramond in Edinburghshire. William de Cramond is designed " Clericus de Warderoba Domini Regis " in a charter of John de Strathern, 1278.

———

DUMBRECK.

Local: from the Castle of Dumbrake in Aberdeenshire.

DURWARD.

See p. 41. Alanus Durward was door ward to Alexander II, who created him Earl of Athol.

———

HALYBURTON.

See p. 54. Sir Walter Halyburton was created Lord Halyburton in 1440.

HERRIES.

Local: from Heries in Normandy. The family are descended from that of Heriz, Lords of Wiverton in Northamptonshire, and were settled in Scotland in the twelfth century — Sir Herbert Herries was created Lord Herries in 1439.

LAMOND.

Originally MacLaman; descended from Laumanus filius Malcolmi, in the thirteenth century.

LOVAT.

Local: from the village of Lovat in Invernesshire.

MACCUITHBERT.

The son of the Arch Druid.

MACINTYRE.

The son of the carpenter.

MACKELLAR.

The son of the steward.

MACLAURIN.

The son of Lawrence.

MACTAGGART.

The son of the priest.

MONYPENNY.

In 1211, Thomas Prior of St. Andrews, gave "Ricardo Monipinii, tenam de Putmullin quam Malisius tenuit." In 1296, John de Monypenny swore fealty to Edward I. In 1335, John de Monypenny was Ambassador from the Pope and French King, to solicit Edward III on behalf of the Scots; and 22d January in that year he obtained a safe conduct to pass into Scotland. Sir William Monypenny was created Lord Monypenny in 1450.

MORLAND.

Local: from the parish of Morland in Westmoreland.

MUIRHEAD.

The head of the Moor.

NICOL.

Descended from Mackrycul, Lord of Assint in Sutherlandshire in the twelfth century.

NIMMO.

Local: from the lands of Nimmo in Stirling-shire.

PARDON.

Local: from the village of Parton in Cumberland.

PETERKIN.

Little Peter.

PRIMROSE.

See p. 86. The family bear three primroses or, in their arms; and for a crest, a demi lion gu., holding a primrose or.

STRAITON.

Local: from the parish of Straiton in Ayr-shire.

STROTHER.

A man of discernment.

———

WHITEFORD.

Local: from the lands of Whiteford in Ren frewshire. The family are descended from Walter de Whiteford, who obtained a grant of the lands from Alexander III, in reward for his courage at the battle of Largs.

DERIVATION

PRINCIPAL CHRISTIAN NAMES

AARON — A mountaineer.

ABEL —Vanity.

ABRAHAM — The father of a great multitude.

ADAM — Man, earthly, red.

ADOLPHUS –- Happy help.

ÆNEAS — Laudable.

ALBERT — Famous.

ALEXANDER —A benefactor.

ALFRED —All peace.

ALISTER — The same as Alexander.

ALLAN — Fair, handsome.

ALWIN —All victorious.

AMBROSE — Immortal.

AMOS —Weighty.

ANDREW —A brave man.

ANGUS — Noble valor.

ANTHONY — Beautiful.
ARCHIBALD — Powerful, bold.
ARNOLD — Honest.
ARTHUR — A strong man.
AUBREY — Always rich.
AUGUSTUS — Noble, royal.
AULAY — A rock.
AUSTIN — Renowned.

ADA — Happiness.
ADELAIDE — Noble.
ADELINE — The same as Adelaide.
AGATHA — Good.
AGNES — Chaste.
ALICE — The same as Adelaide.
AMY — Beloved.
ANNE — Gracious.
ARABELLA — A fair altar.

BALDWIN — The speedy conqueror.
BANE — White, fair, pale.
BANQUO — A white dog.
BARDULPH — Fair help.
BARTHOLOMEW — A son that suspends the waters.
BASIL — Royal, kingly.
BENEDICT — Blessed.
BENJAMIN — The son of the right hand.
BENNET — The same as Benedict.
BERNARD — Child-like.

BERTRAM — Fair and pure.
BOTOLPH — A sailor.
BRIAN — Nobly descended.

BARBARA — A barbarian.
BEATRICE — Blessed, happy.
BERTHA — Bright and famous.
BLANCHE — White, fair.
BRIDGET — A hostage.

CAMUS — A harbor.
CARADOX — Dearly beloved.
CHARLES — Courageous.
CHRISTIAN — A Christian.
CHRISTOPHER — Christ's carrier.
CLARENCE — Clear, bright.
CLAUDE — A weeping voice.
CLEMENT — Gentle, kind.
COLIN — A darling.
CONRAD — Able counsel.
CRINAU — A mournful tune.
CUTHBERT — Famous, bright, of clear skill or knowledge.

CAROLINE — The feminine of Charles.
CATHARINE — Pure, chaste.
CECILIA — Grey-eyed.
CHARLOTTE — The feminine of Charles.
CHRISTINE — The feminine of Christian.

CLARA — Clear, bright.
CLAUDIA — The feminine of Claude.
CLEMENTINE — The feminine of Clement.
CONSTANCE — Constant, firm.

DANIEL — The judgment of God.
DAVID — Beloved.
DENIS — Holy minded.
DONALD — A great chief.
DOUGALL — The black stranger.
DUNCAN — The chieftain's castle.
DUNSTAN — A stony hill.

DEBORAH — A bee.
DELIA — Conspicuous.
DIANA — Jove's daughter.
DORCAS — A doe.

EDGAR — Happy, blessed.
EDMUND — Blessed peace.
EDULPH — The same as Adolphus.
EDWARD — Good nature.
EDWIN — Blessed conqueror.
EGBERT — Always famous.
ENOS — Mortal.
ENRIQUE — The same as Henry.
ERNEST — Earnest.
ETHAN — Strength.
ETHELARD — Noble disposition.

ETHELBERT — Nobly renowned.
ETHELSTAN — Most noble.
ETHELWARD — Noble keeper.
ETHELWOLD — Noble governor.
ETHELWOLF — Noble helper.
EUGENE — Nobly born.
EUSTACE — Resolute.
EVERARD — Always honored.

EDITH — Happiness.
ELEANOR — Compassionate.
ELIZABETH — The oath of God.
ELSIE — The same as Alice.
EMILY — The same as Emmeline.
EMMA — Industrious.
EMMELINE — Little Emma.
ESTHER — Secret.
ETHEL — Noble.
EUGENIA — The feminine of Eugene.
EVA — Life-giving.

FARQUHAR — An honest man.
FELIX — Happy.
FERDINAND — Pure peace.
FERGUS — A brave chieftain.
FRANCIS — Free.
FREDERICK — Rich peace.
FULBERT — Full-bright.
FULKE — Beloved of the people.

FANNY —A corruption of Frances.
FELICIA — The feminine of Felix.
FLORENCE — Flourishing.
FRANCES — The feminine of Francis.

GABRIEL —A man of God.
GEOFFREY — In God secure.
GEORGE —A husbandman.
GERARD — Natural.
GERVAS — Steadfast.
GIFFORD — Liberal.
GILBERT — Bright pledge.
GILCHRIST — The servant of Christ.
GILES — A companion.
GILLEAN —A servant.
GILLEBRIDE — The servant of St. Bridget.
GODARD — Good natured.
GODFREY — Godly.
GODFRIDUS — The same as Godfrey.
GODWIN — Converted to God.
GOSPATRICK — Count Patrick.
GREGOR —A herdsman.
GREGORY —Watchful.
GUAIRE — The same as Godfrey.
GUY —A leader.

GEORGIANA — The feminine of George.
GERTRUDE —Amiable.
GILLIAN — The feminine of Julius.

GRACE — Graceful.

GRISHILD — Grey lady.

HARALD — Leader of the army.

HECTOR — A defender.

HENRY — A rich lord.

HENGIST — A horseman.

HERBERT — A good soldier.

HILDEBERT — A famous lord.

HORACE — Of good eyesight.

HUBERT — Bright color.

HUGH — Exalted.

HUMPHREDUS — The same as Humphrey.

HUMPHREY — House peace.

HANNAH — Merciful.

HARRIET — The feminine of Henry.

HELEN — Compassionate.

HENRIETTA — The feminine of Henry.

HONORA — Honorable.

INGRAHAM — Pure as an angel.

ISAAC — Laughter.

IVER — A chief.

IDA — The same as Edith.

ISABELLA — Olive complexioned.

JACOB — He that supplants.

JAMES — The same as Jacob.

JASPER — Precious.

JEREMIAH — The grandeur of the Lord.

JEROME — The same as Jeremiah.

JOB — He that weeps.

JOEL — One that commands.

JOHN — God's grace.

JONAS — A dove.

JONATHAN — The same as John.

JOSCELYN — A diminutive of Justin.

JOSEPH — Increase.

JOSHUA — The Saviour.

JOSIAH — The fire of the Lord.

JULIUS — Soft haired.

JUSTIN — Just.

JANE — The feminine of John.

JANET — Little Jane.

JEMIMA — Handsome.

JOSEPHINE — The feminine of Joseph.

JUDITH — Praising.

JULIA — The feminine of Julius.

KENARD — Kind-hearted.

KENHELM — A defender of his family.

KENNETH — A chieftain.

KATHARINE — Pure, chaste.

KATHLEEN — Little darling.

LAMBERT — A beautiful lamb.
LAWRENCE — Flourishing.
LEGER — Swift, nimble.
LEMUEL — God is with them.
LEOD — A wounder.
LEOFSTAN — Most beloved.
LEOFWIN — Win love.
LEONARD — Lion-like.
LEOPOLD — A defender of the people.
LEWIS — The safeguard of the people.
LIONEL — A little lion.
LUCAS — Luminous.
LUCIUS — Light.
LUTHER — Fortune and honor.

LAURA — The feminine of Lawrence.
LETITIA — Mirth.
LOUISA — The feminine of Lewis.
LUCRETIA — A good housewife.
LUCY — Bright.

MALCOLM — The servant of Columba.
MARK — Shining.
MARMADUKE — Mighty.
MARTIN — Warlike.
MATTHEW — The gift of God.
MAURICE — A warrior.
MICHAEL — Who is like God?
MILES — A corruption of Michael.
MOSES — Drawn forth.

MABEL—Amiable.

MADELINE — The same as Adeline.

MAGDALEN — Majestical.

MARGARET — Precious.

MARIA — The same as Mary.

MARION — The same as Mary.

MARTHA — Bitter.

MARY — Exalted.

MATILDA — A noble lady.

MAUD — A corruption of Matilda.

MELICENT — Sweet.

MIRIAM — Affliction.

NATHAN — Given.

NATHANIEL — The gift of God.

NEIL — Dark complexion.

NICHOLAS — Victorious.

NIGEL — Swarthy.

NOEL — Christmas.

NORMAN — A native of Normandy.

NANCY — A corruption of Ann.

NANNETTE — Little Anne.

OLIVER — Peace.

OSBERN — An adopted child.

OSBERT — Domestic brightness.

OSMUND — House peace.

OSWALD — A steward.

OWEN — The good offspring.

OLIVIA — The feminine of Oliver.

PATRICK — A senator.
PAUL — Little, small.
PETER — A rock.
PHARLAN — The same as Bartholomew.
PHERSON — A parson.
PHILEBERT — Very famous.
PHILEMON — Loving.
PHILIP — A lover of horses.

PAULINE — The feminine of Paul.
PHILLIPA — The feminine of Philip
PHŒBE — Radiant.
PRISCILLA — An ancient dame.

QUINTIN — The fifth born.

RADULPUS — The same as Ralph.
RALPH — A counsellor.
RANDAL — The same as Randolph.
RANDOLPH — Fair help.
RANULPH — The same as Randolph.
RAYMOND — Pure mouth.
REGINALD — King-like.
REYNARD — Incorrupt.
REYNOLD — Pure love.
RICHARD — Of a generous disposition.

ROBERT — Famous in council.
RODERICK — Rich in counsel.
ROGER — Peace.
ROLAND — Counsel for the land.
RUEL — God's shepherd.
RUFUS — Red.
RUPERT — The same as Robert.

RACHEL — A sheep.
REBECCA — Fat.
REGINA — Queen-like.
RHODA — A rose.
ROSALIE — Fair as a rose.
ROSALIND — The same as Rosalie.
ROSAMOND — Rosy lips.
ROWENA — Acquired peace.
RUTH — Satisfied.

SAMUEL — A prophet.
SEBASTIAN — Majestical.
SIGEBERT — Victorious fame.
SIGISMUND — Victorious peace.
SIMON — Hearing.
STEPHEN — Honor.
SWITHIN — Very high.
SYLVESTER — A woodman.

SARAH — Mistress.
SOPHIA — Wisdom.
SYBIL — God's counsel.

THEOBALD — Bold over the people.
THEODORE — The gift of God.
THEODORIC — Rich in people.
THOMAS — A twin.
TIMOTHY — One who honors God.
TOBIAS — The goodness of God.
TRISTRAM — Sad.

THEODOSIA — The feminine of Theodore.

UMPHRED — The same as Humphrey.
UTHRED — High counsel.

URSULA — A little bear.

VALENTINE — Brave.
VICTOR — A conqueror.
VINCENT — Victorious.

VIOLA — Pretty and modest.
VIRGINIA — Maidenly.

WALDEN — A wood.
WALTER — The lord of the wood.
WIBERT — Holy and bright.
WILDRED — Great fear.
WILFRED — Much peace.
WILLIAM — A defence of many.

WIMUND — Sacred peace.
WOLSTAN — Comely.
WULPHER — A helper.

WILHELMINA — The feminine of William.
WINIFRED — Get peace.

ZACHARIAH — The memory of the Lord.